The New Novello Choral Edition
NOVELLO HANDEL EDITION

General Editor   Donald Burrows

Ode for Saint Cecilia's Day
(HWV 76)

ST or SAT soloists, SATB chorus and orchestra

Edited by Donald Burrows

Vocal Score

Order No: NOV720071

NOVELLO PUBLISHING LIMITED
14 - 15 Berners Street, London, W1T 3LJ

CONTENTS

Approximate duration
27 minutes

INSTRUMENTATION

Flute
2 Oboes
2 Bassoons
2 Trumpets
Timpani
Strings
Continuo (Harpsichord, Organ, and optional Lute)

The performing material for this edition includes two fully-realised parts, Continuo 1 (Harpsichord) and Continuo 2 (Organ), prepared in accordance with Handel's practice. The Organ is specifically required for Nos. 7(A or B) and 9, as well as fulfilling a continuo role in the chorus movements. The Lute part in No. 7 is also included in the Harpsichord part, for alternative use when no Lute is available.

PREFACE

Handel composed the Ode between 15 and 24 September 1739 and it was first performed, with *Alexander's Feast*, on 22 November (St. Cecilia's Day). The London celebrations of St Cecilia's Day in the latter years of the seventeenth century had regularly included musical settings of specially-written odes. John Dryden was responsible for two of them: *Alexander's Feast* in 1697, originally set to music by Jeremiah Clarke, and the shorter *Song for St Cecilia's Day, 1687*, set by Giovanni Battista Draghi. Both of these were published at the time as literary texts. For Handel's version of *Alexander's Feast* in 1736, Dryden's text was adapted by Newburgh Hamilton to provide the structures for recitatives, arias and chorus movements appropriate to the style of English works that the composer had developed. It may also have been Hamilton who directed Handel's attention to Dryden's shorter ode, as a possible complement to *Alexander's Feast*. The latter had been composed as a two-part work, but the London theatre audiences expected a three-act evening, so Dryden's ode provided an independent one-act piece that could be coupled with it. This also had a happy result in an attractive shorter repertory piece that can be accommodated to present-day concert programmes.

22 November 1739 was the opening night of Handel's theatre season of 1739-40: a season that we would now regard as historically significant, because it was the first one in which he presented entirely English works, performed as concert pieces in the 'oratorio' manner. At the time, the composer was making the best of his current situation. On the one hand, he had suffered in recent years through the competitive chaos caused by the existence of two Italian opera companies in London: in 1739-40 he did not have the resources to present an opera programme himself, and he resorted to hiring the old theatre at Lincoln's Inn Fields, a less fashionable venue than the King's Theatre in the Haymarket or the new theatre at Covent Garden, at which he had performed in recent years. On the other hand, he was at that time developing a new relationship with the London audience through performances of English works, and through collaboration with the music publisher John Walsh, which had recently resulted in a handsome full score edition of *Alexander's Feast*.

Between the composition of the Ode and its first performance Handel composed a set of twelve orchestral concertos. These were performed with his theatre works, but they were also published as his 'Grand Concertos' Op. 6 in April 1740. For one of these concertos (Op. 6 No. 5) he based the opening two movements on the Ouverture that he had written at the start of the Ode. For his compositions at this period he drew on musical ideas from two published collections of keyboard music: Domenico Scarlatti's *Essercizi* for the concertos, and Gottlieb Muffat's *Componimenti Musicali* for the Ode. The scale passages from one movement by Muffat proved especially apposite for 'Through all the compass of the notes it ran'.

Confusion over the title of Handel's work began with the composer himself. At the beginning of the autograph score he at first wrote 'Ouverture to the Song for St Cecilia's Day Ode by Mr Dryden. 1687', and then altered this to 'Ouverture to the Song for St Cecilia's Day by Mr Dryden. 1687'. The printed librettos for Handel's performances head the text 'A Song for St Cecilia's Day', but even in the first advertisements for his performances it is referred to as an 'ode'; furthermore, several early musical sources call it the 'Ode for St Cecilia's Day', and that is the title by which it has become generally known. Since Dryden's longer Cecilian ode is *Alexander's Feast*, the title 'Ode for St Cecilia's Day' is unambiguous for the present work, and need not be regarded as incorrect.

Beyond the initial performances in 1739, Handel revived the Ode several times, usually in association with a two-part work. In the first season, after two performances with *Alexander's Feast*, it was coupled with *Acis and Galatea*, as it was also in Handel's following London season, and again for his performances at Dublin in 1742. On returning to London, Handel coupled the Ode with *L'Allegro ed Il Penseroso* for his Covent Garden oratorio season in 1743, and this combination, presenting in one evening his settings of texts by Milton and Dryden, was revived in 1754 and 1755. Inevitably changes in his cast of soloists from year to year involved various amendments: in 1741, for example, Handel provided an alternative Italian text to No. 8 for the castrato singer Andreoni. Overall, however, the musical structure of the work remained remarkably stable through the various revivals. The biggest changes took place between the draft composition of the score and the first performance: Handel originally composed No. 5 as an aria (as it was published in the printed edition of songs from the Ode), but before the first performance he added the chorus and the following March, No. 6.

There are, however, some variants from Handel's performances that are included in this edition and may be considered by present-day performers. For the 1739 performances Handel employed just two soloists, a tenor and a soprano. When he had more high-register soloists available in subsequent seasons, he divided the soprano arias between different singers, and even re-allocated a tenor aria (No. 8) to one of them, presumably singing the music an octave higher. For the London performances in 1743 he composed an alto-voice version of No. 7 (here No. 7B) for Mrs Cibber, and this was used again during the 1750s for the castrato singer Guadagni.[1] In No. 12 Handel shortened the movement in the performing score with a substantial cut from bar 84 to bar 145. This was probably done to shorten the overall evening when the Ode was combined with other works, but we do not know when the cut was made or whether Handel retained it for all subsequent performances. (All of the early secondary manuscripts have the full form of the movement, suggesting that the cut was not a feature of the score in the early years.) Since the excised section provides contrasted excursions to different keys, it seems more appropriate to perform the longer version when the Ode is given as a free-standing work, but there is no doubt that the shorter version also has the composer's authority as an alternative.[2]

The other choices concern the Ouverture, and here our evidence about Handel's performances is lacking. The conducting score now begins with No. 2: we do not know if it was always thus, but three secondary manuscript sources that were otherwise derived from that score include the original Ouverture. In view of the mention of 'two new Concerto's for Instruments' in the advertisements for the first performance of the Ode, it seems very likely that the concerto Op. 6 No. 5 might have been played instead of Handel's original Ouverture. (It is unlikely that any concerto was performed in the course of the Ode itself.) We do not know what Handel performed in subsequent revivals and, since Op. 6 No. 5 now has an independent existence as an orchestral work, it is logical to return to the overture that he intended for the Ode. Even so, the sources provide three different versions of the Menuet. In Handel's autograph score the Ouverture had originally concluded with a bipartite movement in D minor and D major (Menuet B), but Handel subsequently deleted the minor-key section, producing Menuet A.[3] A further complication is introduced by the Ouverture as printed in the first published edition of the complete score (Source **WR**), which has only the D major movement, but in the more extended version as found in Op. 6 No. 5 (Menuet C). This was not published with the Ode until 1771, and may reflect the way that the Ouverture was performed in the years after Handel's death, but there is also the possibility that it preserves an older tradition going back to the composer himself. The Ode is unusual in that it was not represented in the collections of Handel's overtures that John Walsh published regularly during the composer's lifetime, as orchestral parts and as keyboard arrangements; this was perhaps on account of the extent of musical duplication with the concerto. In the absence of firm evidence about the version, or versions, of the Ouverture that Handel performed in the Ode, all three alternatives are provided here.

SOME PRACTICAL CONSIDERATIONS
RHYTHMIC ALTERATION
Handel's notation is presented as the music text. Editorial suggestions for rhythmic modifications, indicated by 'flags', have been added to cover two contexts: places where the last note of a phrase needs to be shortened in order to clear a harmonic change, and places where a rhythm may be amended to conform to the movement of other parts or the prevailing pattern. A cautious approach has been taken to the latter, and performers may well wish to extend the principle elsewhere. The extent of the regularisation that may have been practised by Handel's performers remains a matter of debate, and the evidence will probably be forever inadequate.
MATTERS FOR SINGERS
Editorial suggestions are given for the application of appoggiaturas at phrase-endings, but the relevant places are few in number: over-use would weaken the declamatory style in Nos. 2 and 11.

In Handel's performances it is very likely that the soloists also sang in the chorus sections.

---

1   Mrs Cibber had sung for Handel at Dublin in 1742, but not until after the end of the first subscription series in which the Ode had been performed.

2   It so happens that the passage that was marked for the cut included a section that Handel had added during composition, probably in order to provide key contrast: bars 127–144 replaced three bars in the first draft of the movement. Handel may also have attempted to compose the chorus to specific proportions, as he wrote the bar numbers '100' at the end of bar 166 and '150' after the final bar.

3   Menuet B was copied into Sources **C** and **M**; Source **F** has Menuet A..

In No. 5, at the link in bars 74-79, Handel wrote rests in the solo part in bars 75-76, but then 'tutti Chorus' in the tenor part at the end of bar 78 and the arrangement of staves in the autograph suggests that this included the soloist. It may be effective to smooth over the join by including the soloist in some of the following music, perhaps bars 82-87.

In No. 2 the conducting score has alternative melodic lines in pencil for the soloist at bars 32-34 and 38-41. These were almost certainly written by Handel in 1743, when this movement was sung by the baritone William Savage, and were probably never used by the tenor soloists in his other performances. The alternative lines are shown as small-size notes.

CONTINUO ACCOMPANIMENT AND RECITATIVES

As will be apparent from small-note passages in the vocal score, some sections of airs are accompanied by the basso continuo only, without upper orchestral instruments. In these passages it may be desirable to reduce the orchestral bass line to a single cello (or one cello and one double bass): in the full score and relevant orchestral parts the continuo-accompanied passages are marked 'Solo'. Accompaniment of *semplice* ('secco') recitatives, and harmonic filling in airs, were the perquisite of the harpsichord: it is uncertain whether a cello also joined in the accompaniment of these recitatives, but provision has been made for this alternative in the orchestral parts. (In the Vocal Score, the accompaniment to the recitatives is designated 'Cont.'.) The notation of *semplice* recitatives involved a long-note convention for the duration of the harmonies, which did not imply that the player(s) had to hold the notes for the full length, or that the harpsichordist could not repeat or decorate the chords within the given framework of voice and accompaniment. The editorial realisation of the recitatives follows a simple style that can be used as the basis for further elaboration, by repeating or decorating the chords, or thickening the texture from time to time; however, the continuo should support the singer without providing a distraction, and enable the text to be delivered effectively. Individual singers may require different forms and levels of support, and the realisations provided should make a flexible basis for this. The harmonic realisation follows the figuring from Handel's bass part, but this is very sporadic and the best guide lies in the harmonic implications of the singers' music.

The basso continuo obviously requires the participation of at least one chord-playing instrument. For the performances of his English oratorio-style works at the relevant period (i.e. from 1739 onwards) Handel used both harpsichord and organ, with clearly defined roles: the harpsichord was the principal accompanying instrument, while the organ provided support to the chorus and was otherwise limited to playing the bass line, *tasto solo*, in sections of some airs and in accompanied recitatives.[4] Since the roles were conventional, the continuo instruments were not normally named by Handel unless some exceptional use was involved, as in Nos. 7 and 9.

Dryden's text refers in turn to the power of different musical instruments to rouse or express the emotions. In both versions of No. 7 the named instruments for 'woes of hopeless lovers' are the flute and the lute, and Handel introduced these into the scoring, with (exceptionally) the organ taking over the continuo role from the harpsichord, beginning at bar 22 in No. 7A and presumably at an equivalent place in No. 7B. The lute music, probably composed for the lutenist Carlo Arrigoni, has a decorative obbligato part from bar 39 onwards in No. 7A, and bar 82 onwards in No. 7B. Handel referred to the instrument as 'Liuto', but the range and the notation indicate the larger Archlute. The lute may also have been employed in other movements as well, though its constant presence would have undermined the particular effect in No. 7. In the performing material for this edition, a figured bass part for the final chorus is included in the lute part, for use *ad libitum*. Since, exceptionally, Handel specified the organ as a keyboard continuo instrument in the relevant sections of No. 7, the lute part may be played on the harpsichord (with appropriate registration) if no lutenist is available. It should be noted also that Handel directed that the violins should be muted ('sordini') in No. 7B, but there is no comparable instruction in No. 7A.

No. 9 is obviously a special case, because the organ is the topic of the text: here Handel wrote out the obbligato part for the organ, while the harpsichord presumably fulfils the regular continuo role, as it does in all of the other movements except No. 7.

---

4 The evidence for the complementary use of the instruments comes from the surviving original performing parts for *Alexander's Feast*: see Donald Burrows, 'Who does what, when', in Richard G. King (ed.), *Handel Studies: A Gedenkschrift for Howard Serwer* (Hillsdale, NY, 2009), pp. 107-26.

This Ode has only two recitatives, Nos. 2 and 11. At the end of both Handel notated delayed cadences, so this work is free from the uncertainties that arise in other works about the treatment of appoggiaturas and cadence chords.

THE ORCHESTRAL ACCOMPANIMENT

Abbreviations at the beginning of each movement indicate the scoring: these are provided to assist the planning of rehearsals. 'Bsn*' indicates that the movement is provided with an editorial Bassoon part. In movements 2 and 9 Handel clearly specified 'Bassons' in his score, but there are no passages with two independent parts. 'Str.' indicates the full string section, except in Nos 7A, 7B and 8, where there are no Violas. Handel's intentions for the scoring of the orchestral accompaniment are unclear only over a few details: the Preface to the full score identifies these, and the editorial choices that have been made.

SOURCES

i) PRINCIPAL MANUSCRIPT SOURCES

A London, British Library, RM 20.f.4. Handel's autograph score, dated 15 September 1739 at the beginning of the Ouverture and 24 September at the end. This is the first score in which Handel added astrological signs for the days of the week to his dates. The chorus section to No. 5, the March No. 6, and an extension to No. 12 (bars 127-144, replacing three bars in the original) were added subsequent to the original drafting, but before the first performance.

A2 Cambridge, Fitzwilliam Museum MU MS 262. A miscellaneous volume of Handel's autograph pages, including short sketches on pp. 61-2 relating to the Ode (Nos 8 and 12) and the Op. 6 Concerti, and a more extended 2-stave draft for No. 6 on p. 64, headed 'March'.

A3 London, British Library, RM 20.g.11, ff. 71-75 and Cambridge, Fitzwilliam Museum MU MS 264, pp. 9-14. Handel's autograph of the Concerto Grosso Op. 6 No. 5, now divided. It includes the Menuet (MS 264, pp. 13-14) in Version C, showing parts for Oboes that were not included in the published edition of Op. 6.

B Hamburg, Staats- und Universitätsbibliothek Carl von Ossietzky, MS M A/1031. Handel's performing score (or 'conducting score'), copied in 1739 by John Christopher Smith the elder. The score now begins with No. 2;

there is an original title for the work on the first page, suggesting that the Ouverture may never have been included. The extension to No. 12 was copied as part of the score, but No. 5 (chorus section) and No. 6 were added as an insertion. For the revival in 1743 a further addition was made, of No. 7B, as an alternative to 7A: this was composed for Mrs Cibber. The names of the original vocal soloists, John Beard and Francesina (Elisabeth Duparc), were copied in 1739 as part of the score, and subsequent names were added by Handel and others in pencil, relating to later revivals. No. 8 has an alternative Italian text in pencil, written by Handel in 1741 for the castrato Andreoni. The shortening of No. 12 (bars 84-144) is indicated with pencil brackets, almost certainly written by Handel and probably added in 1741. No movements have transposition directions, but names of soloists written by Handel on No. 8 include those of the soprano-register singers Andreoni and Mrs Clive.

ii) SECONDARY MANUSCRIPT COPIES

C Manchester Public Library, Henry Watson Music Library, MS 130 Hd4 v.187. Full score, from the Aylesford Collection, copied by J. C. Smith the elder for Charles Jennens, c.1740, bound in a volume with two other scores, including movements from Handel's pasticcio opera *Jupiter in Argos* (1739).

D London, Foundling Museum, Gerald Coke Handel Collection 636. Full score, from the Shaftesbury Collection, the work of two copyists (S4A and S4B), c.1740.[5] This score and **E** were presumably originally copied for the 4th Earl of Shaftesbury.

E London, Foundling Museum, Gerald Coke Handel Collection 637. Full score, from the Shaftesbury Collection, in the hand of copyist S2, c.1740.

F Cambridge, Fitzwilliam Museum MU MS 794. Full score, from the 'Lennard Collection', in the hand of copyist S5, with two pages in the hand of S7 (James Hunter),

---

5 For the 'S' classification of Handel's music copyists, see Jens Peter Larsen, *Handel's 'Messiah': Origins, Composition, Sources* (London, 1957), Chapter 4. A number of different copyists have subsequently been grouped with 'S4', and for the present purpose these have been designated 'S4A' and 'S4B'.

in a volume with *Alexander's Feast*.[6] Copied *c*.1741.

G   London, Foundling Museum, Gerald Coke Handel Collection 728. Full score in the hand of copyist S5, in a volume with Handel's *L'Allegro* and other material, copied *c*. 1741.

H   Durham Cathedral Library MS E23. Full score of Nos. 3 and 12, in the hand of an unidentified copyist, with an accompanying set of part-books (six vocal parts, Violin 1 and Cembalo), written by three copyists including Richard Fawcett and William Walond senior.[7] The part-books originated from performers who were active in Oxford during the 1740s: the Violin 1 part-book has, as a cover, pages from a newspaper dated 5 January 1742. A list on the cover-sheet to the MS indicates that the set originally comprised the following: Violin 1 (2 copies), Violin 2 (2 copies), Viola, Cello obbligato, Cello ripieno, Contra Basso, Oboe 1, Oboe 2, Bassoon obbligato, Canto [Soprano], Alto, Tenor (2 copies), Bass (2 copies) and '1 Basso in Score with Violoncello Rep[ieno]' The choruses may have been performed separately, or they may have been copied to complement the movements from **W**, in order to provide a complete performable version of the Ode.

J   Princeton University Library, New Jersey, U.S.A., James S. Hall Collection, Volume 4. Full score of Nos. 2, 3, 11 and 12, in the hand of an unidentified copyist, in a volume with Handel's Ode for Queen Anne's Birthday (HWV 74) and other material. Date uncertain, but possibly from the early 1740s. As with source **H**, this was probably copied to complement the music that was available from **W**. The score has some serious copying errors, some of which were subsequently corrected.

K   London, British Library RM 19.a.2, ff. 47-51. Score of No. 7B, written by an unidentified copyist *c*.1743-4 in a

volume, from the Aylesford Collection, of miscellaneous movements by Handel, many of them composed later in the decade. Copied for Charles Jennens, who described this movement on the contents page of the volume as 'Aria in Mr Dryden's Ode'.

L   Bethlehem, Pennsylvania, U.S.A., Moravian Archives, vol. 17. A volume comprising music from several of Handel's works in score, written in an economical manner on folio-format pages.[8] On ff. 105-110 the complete contents of **W** were copied ('Songs in ye Ode for St. Cecilia's Day by Mr Dryden Da G: F Handel'), and dated May 1740 at the end by the copyist; later, on ff. 140-150, the remaining movements apart from the Ouverture and No. 7B were copied ('Suplement to ye New Cæcelia's Ode'), dated 1744 at the end, and cues were added between the two sections to show the sequence of the complete score.

M   Manchester Public Library, Henry Watson Music Library, MS 130 Hd4 vv.112-3, 155, 214-224. Parts, vocal and instrumental, for 'Dryden's Song for St. Cecilia's Day', in part-books copied for Charles Jennens in the later 1740s, but never used for performance. From the Aylesford Collection, and probably derived from Source **C**.

N   Dublin, Archbishop Marsh's Library, St Patrick's Cathedral, Z 1.2.27. Full score, using pages of the printed edition **W**, supplemented by manuscript pages to give the complete work except for the Ouverture. Copied by John Mathews, Lay Vicar of Salisbury Cathedral, and dated by him 20th June 1764.

O   London, British Library, RM 18.c.6. Full score, copied in 1765 by S10. From the 'Smith Collection', possibly copied for King George III.

P   London, Royal College of Music, MS 253. Full score, copied *c*.1765 by an unidentified copyist. Formerly from the collection of the Concerts of Antient Music.

Q   Manchester Public Library, Henry Watson Music Library, MS 130 Hd4 v.314, p. 169. No. 6 ('March by Handell in St. Cicely's

6   See Ellen T. Harris, 'James Hunter, Handel's Friend', *Händel-Jahrbuch* Jg. 46 (2000), pp. 247-64, and Donald Burrows, 'Something necessary to the connection': Charles Jennens, James Hunter and Handel's *Samson*', *The Handel Institute Newsletter* 15/1 (Spring 2004), pp. 1-3.

7   See Peter Ward Jones and Donald Burrows, 'An inventory of mid-eighteenth-century Oxford musical hands', *Royal Musical Association Research Chronicle* 35 (2002), pp. 61-144.

8   This is the only source that has not been examined at first hand for the preparation of this edition; the volume could not be found when I visited Bethlehem in 2007, but a microfilm was available. Related volumes (containing music from Handel's operas) are now in the Gerald Coke Handel Collection (London), the Staatsbibliothek (Berlin), and the Library of Congress (Washington D.C.).

Ode') as a 2-stave version, probably for keyboard, in a volume of miscellaneous pieces formerly owned by Edward Weld of Lulworth Castle, Dorset. Copyist unknown, but the music was derived from **W**, possibly c.1740-1.

iii) PRINTED MUSIC EDITIONS

W *The Songs in the Ode wrote by Mr. Dryden for St. Cecilia's Day Set by Mr. Handel. London Printed for & Sould by I: Walsh* [December 1739] 23 pp., comprising Nos. 4, 5 (air only), 6, 7A, 8, 9 and 10. The singers are named for each vocal item: 'Sigra. Francesina' for Nos. 4, 7A, 9 and 10, 'Mr. Beard' for Nos. 5 and 8.

WS *Sonatas or Chamber Aires for a German Flute Violin or Harpsichord … Vol. IV Part 4th Printed for & Sold by I. Walsh* [January 1740] 25 pp., of which pp. 2-17 have reduced-score instrumental arrangements of Nos. 4, 5 (aria only), 6, 7A, 8 (in G major) and 10 (in E minor); the remainder of the volume has movements from Handel's *Il Trionfo del Tempo*.

WC *Twelve Grand Concertos in Seven Parts …By George Frederick Handel. Publish'd by the Author. London Printed for and Sold by Iohn Walsh* [April 1740]; 'Opera Sexta' was added to the title page for the Second Edition (1741). The original edition of Handel's Op. 6 concertos, including Op. 6 No. 5 with music related to the Ouverture of the Ode.

WF *The Musick for the Royal Fireworks Set for a German Flute Violin or Harpsichord Compos'd By Mr. Handel London. Printed for I Walsh* [July 1749] Following the *Fireworks Music*, this has a collection of other movements by Handel including No. 6 from the Ode on p. 11, without the name of the work. **WS** and **WF** were derived from **W**, having the same erroneous bass note at the start of bar 5.

WR *The Complete Score of the Ode for St: Cecilia's Day the Words by Mr. Dryden, Set to Music by Mr. Handel …London Printed for William Randall (Successor to the late Mr. I. Walsh)* [1771]. Unlike many of Randall's editions, this one did not use any plates from the preceding Walsh edition of the Songs, but was newly engraved throughout.

iv) LIBRETTO SOURCES

L1 Printed word-book, *Alexander's Feast; or, the Power of Musick. An Ode. Wrote on Honour of St. Cecilia, And a Song for St. Cecilia's Day.* *Both written by Mr. Dryden. And Set to Musick by Mr. Handel. … London: Printed for J. and R. Tonson in the Strand. MDCCXXXIX* [1739] 20 pp., with the 'Song' on pp. 17-20.

L2 Printed word-book, *The Masque of Acis and Galatea. The Musick By Mr. Handell. Printed in the Year MDCCXLII* [Dublin, 1742] 21 pp., with the heading 'A Song for St Cecilia's Day. Written by Mr. Dryden' on p. 17, and the text on pp. 17-21.

L3 Printed word-book, *L'Allegro, ed Il Penseroso. By Milton. And a Song for St. Cecilia's Day. By Dryden. Set to Musick by George Frederick Handel. London: Printed for J. and R. Tonson in the Strand. MDCCXLIII* [1743]. 20 pp., with the 'Song' on pp. 17-20. There is also a version with the same pagination, dated *MDCCLIV* [1754]. These are the word-books from Handel's performances, though there is some doubt about his involvement in the 1754 event. The text of the 'Song' is identical in all of the books, apart from minor variants such as 'power' for 'pow'r, and the airs are numbered 1-6.

L0 ' *A Song for St. Cecilia's Day, 1687. Written by John Dryden, Esq; And Compos'd by Mr. John Baptist Draghi*', pp. 242-6 in *Examen Poeticum: being the Third Part of Miscellany Poems …by the Most Eminent Hands* (London, 1683). The original text of Dryden's ode, in seven numbered stanzas and concluding with 'As from the pow'r of sacred Lays [etc.]' under the heading 'Grand Chorus'. (This heading was repeated in Handel's word-books.) The structure and content are identical to Handel's text, except that Handel set Stanza 7 as two separate movements, Nos. 10 and 11.

EDITORIAL PRACTICE

The main sources for this edition are MSS **A** and **B**. **K** provides another contemporary copy of No. 7B, which is found in **B**, but for which there is no surviving composer's autograph. **C**, **F**, **M** and **WR** include the Ouverture, which is not found in **B**. Otherwise, all of the secondary MSS are derived from the present musical text of **B** as it stood before the insertion of No. 7B. Obvious errors in transcription from **A** to **B** have been tacitly corrected, and authentic amendments that were executed only in **B** have been tacitly adopted. The few significant differences between musical readings in these sources are noted in the full score to this edition. The overall form of the work as presented by Handel remained basically unchanged from the first performances in 1739 through to his last revival in 1755, so the relevant libretto sources have identical texts.

Clefs have been modernised for the vocal parts: the original clefs were soprano (C1) for soprano voices, alto (C3) for alto voices, and tenor (C4) for tenor voices. Barring has been regularised in a few places, principally in the final bars of No. 12, where Handel wrote the long chords as breves.

Handel's system for accidentals has been modernised (with consequential modification to the figurings in the full score), and small-size accidentals are used where he may have omitted an intended inflection. Minor amendments to the music where Handel may have overlooked momentary errors are recorded in footnotes.

Movement numberings are editorial. Libretto sources have been regarded as authoritative for details of the verbal text, but not followed slavishly; punctuation and spellings from the principal musical and libretto sources have been modernised, but apparently deliberate word-forms have been retained.

Conventional pause signs indicating movement endings have been removed: in *da capo* or *dal segno* movements these are replaced by 'Fine'. Handel's slurs in the vocal parts to indicate word-underlay have been omitted, and his note-beaming has been modernised; slurs from the principal sources for the orchestral parts are included. Editorial suggestions for additional dynamics, tempo directions, staccato dashes, trills, etc. are shown in square brackets, and editorial slurs or ties are shown thus: ⌢. In the vocal score, continuous groups of obvious *simile* slurs and staccato dashes are not indicated as editorial unless there is some anomaly in the pattern; in the full score all such marks that do not have authority from **A** or **B** are shown as editorial. The *hemiola*, or conventional cadential rhythmic re-grouping in triple time, is indicated by horizontal square brackets thus: ⌐‾‾‾⌐‾‾‾⌐‾‾‾⌐. Editorial suggestions for rhythmic modification are shown by 'flags' above or below the stave or stave-system: see above, 'Rhythmic Alteration'.

The keyboard accompaniment is a practical reduction of the principal activity in the orchestral parts, suitable for rehearsal accompaniment. The harmonic bass line is preserved as the lowest part; 'Senza DB.' indicates orchestral passages without double bass, and 'Bassi' indicates subsequent re-entries; 'Cont.' indicates passages accompanied by the Continuo, including those where Handel's bass line shows the doubling of upper parts without the participation of orchestral bass instruments. Editorial continuo realisation is shown in small-size notes, and these are also used for additional details of the orchestral texture which can be included in some circumstances (e.g. in No.2 bar 12). In some places the pianist may have to abandon a sustained bass part in order to maintain an element of the texture above: where there is a clash of musical priorities, notes that are literal but unplayable are shown in round brackets. Realisations have taken account of Handel's intermittent continuo figurings. Indications for trills from the sources are included, but not all may be practical for the keyboard accompaniment (as, for example the first one in bar 19 of the Ouverture, or those in bars 7-8 of No. 5); in many places Handel's standard 'tr' marking indicates a short ornament. In the interests of rhythmic clarity, pianists may also wish to simplify the rhythms in the bass part in No. 5 bars 11-12 and No. 12 bars 183-4.

ACKNOWLEDGEMENTS

I extend my grateful thanks to the owners and curators of the sources for this edition, for facilitating access to the original materials, and also to John Greenacombe for information about the word-books. Research for the edition, and initial preparation of the music text by Blaise Compton, was supported by the Arts Faculty at The Open University. I thank those involved in the production of this edition, in particular Howard Friend and Hywel Davies from Novello Publishing.

Donald Burrows, 2009

ODE FOR SAINT CECILIA'S DAY

ODE FOR SAINT CECILIA'S DAY

John Dryden
A Song for Saint Cecilia's Day 1687

GEORGE FRIDERIC HANDEL
HWV 76

No.1

OUVERTURE

2

4

Menuet A

Obs,
Bsn*, Str.

Segue No.2 (p.6)

Menuet B

Vlns

Obs,
Bsn*, Str.

Vla, Vc.

Senza DB

Segue Menuet A

Menuet C

Un poco larghetto

Obs,
Bsn*, Str.

* BC notes written by Handel an octave higher

Recitative and Accompanied Recitative FROM HARMONY
Tenor

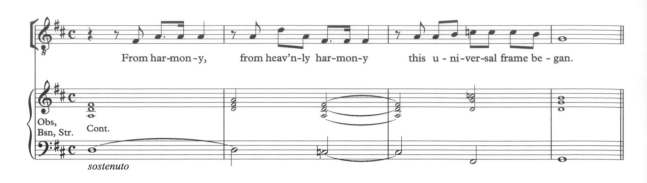

From har-mon-y, from heav'n-ly har-mon-y this u-ni-ver-sal frame be-gan.

Obs, Bsn, Str.   Cont.

sostenuto

Larghetto e piano

When na-ture un-der-neath a heap Of jar-ring a-toms

Obs, Bsn, Str.

p

[*sim.*]

lay, when na-ture un-der-neath a

heap of jar-ring a-toms lay, And could not heave her head,

8

then cold   and hot,   and moist   and dry,   in or - der   to their sta - tions

leap,

And mu - sic's pow'r o -

-bey,   and mu - sic's pow'r o - bey.

* Alternative notes were added in pencil, probably by Handel, in **B**; see Preface.

No.3   Chorus FROM HARMONY, FROM HEAV'NLY HARMONY

Chorus

10

12

[senza DB]   [Tutti]

No.4   Air WHAT PASSION CANNOT MUSIC RAISE AND QUELL?
Soprano

* In the keyboard accompaniment for this movement, it is suggested that the tied notes in BC passages marked [ ] be omitted.
† Possibly with Oboes: see Preface

18

on their fa - - ces fell To wor - ship that ce - les - tial

sound, to wor - ship that ce - les - tial sound.

Less than a god they thought

there could not dwell With - in the hol - low

of that shell, That spoke so sweet - ly and so well.

mu - sic raise and quell? What pas-sion can-not mu - sic

Vc. solo

146 adagio [a tempo]

raise_____ and quell?

Vlns

[*f*]

Vc. solo

151

[*mf*]

[*p*]

[Tutti]

157 ad libitum [a tempo]

Vlns

[*mf*]

f

163 Tutti

No.5   Solo and Chorus **THE TRUMPET'S LOUD CLANGOUR**

Tenor solo and Chorus

The trum-pet's loud clang-our ex - cites us to arms,   ex-

-cites us to arms,   to arms, to arms, the trum-pet's loud clang-our ex - cites us to arms,

* **A** and **B** have different rhythms for Timpani in bars 43-4.

24

* The soloist may continue with chorus Tenors: see Preface.

No.6   LA MARCHE

Segue either No.7A (p.28) or No.7B (p.32)

No.7A   Air   THE SOFT COMPLAINING FLUTE
                          Soprano

Segue No.8 (p.37)

No.7B   Air   THE SOFT COMPLAINING FLUTE (alternative setting)

Alto

The soft com - plain

No.8 Air SHARP VIOLINS PROCLAIM
Tenor

Sharp vi - o-lins pro-claim Their jea - lous pangs and des-pe-ra - tion,

pas - sion for the fair dis - dain - ful dame, for the_

fair dis-dain-ful_ dame, for the fair_ dis-dain - ful

dame.

Air BUT OH! WHAT ART CAN TEACH
Soprano

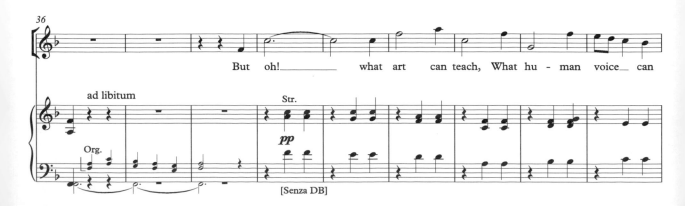

But oh!_____ what art can teach, What hu - man voice_ can

[Senza DB]

* Handel included this passage in the BC part, probably an oversight.

† Handel wrote 'to choirs above'.

44

No.10   Air ORPHEUS COULD LEAD THE SAVAGE RACE
Soprano

No.11   Accompanied Recitative BUT BRIGHT CECILIA

Soprano

Solo and Chorus: AS FROM THE POW'R OF SACRED LAYS
Soprano and Chorus

50

un poco più Allegro

[Senza DB]

* Optional cut to bar 145: see Preface

53

* f' in **A** and **B**

62